The Art of Living
30 Day Inspirational

Terry A. Weems, Sr.

THE ART OF LIVING

30 Day Inspirational

Copyright © 2017, Terry A. Weems, Sr.

Editing by Renae Sellers

Book Design by Robert Matthews

ISBN-13: 978-1985389458

ISBN-10: 1985389452

Dedication

This book is dedicated to those who give
their lives for the sake of others as religious,
political and community leaders.

Preface

The parable of the prodigal son is the story of a man filled with internal deficits. These deficits could have developed from rejection, neglect, and abandonment which could have contributed to his attraction to a foreign country; ultimately resulting in a climate of riotous living. It was not until he realized the void of his existence that he was able to come to his senses and return to a life of abundance. (Luke 15:11-32)

'The Art of Living' requires that you be liberated from places that appear to be comfortable but are detrimental to your destiny. A change in mentality creates an atmosphere of enjoyment, exultation, and elation. Live your best life NOW!

Day 1 - 'Art Speaks'

Art speaks of the science of creative imagination. God's creative imagination brought earth and life into being. Life can be compared to an orange where layers have to be peeled so that the fruit can be discovered. Each moment represents an opportunity to unearth hidden treasure so the fruit of the Spirit can be revealed.

Life Application

Today, begin the process of peeling off layers of emotional baggage, old patterns of behavior, old mindsets, and cycles of failure. Today is the day to discover the rich internal resources that lie within you. You have it in you to pursue your passion and leave the baggage behind.

Biblical Reflection

"But the Holy Spirit produces this kind of fruit in our lives: love, joy, peace, patience, kindness, goodness, faithfulness, gentleness, and self-control. There is no law against these things!"
Galatians 5:22-23 (NLT)

Day 2 - 'You Are Victorious'

Daily Inspiration

No one is exempt from the variations of life's twist and turns. You must know how to navigate through turbulence, trauma, and transition as you encounter surprises, uncertainties, and difficulties. You must have the capacity to quickly recover from circumstances that altar your perception. It is not what is happening to you but your perception of what is happening to you that makes the difference.

Life Application

Practice quietness and stillness. Tap inside of you for solutions to life's problems. Encourage yourself! Speak life into your situation and tell yourself today, "I am VICTORIOUS!"

Biblical Reflection

"Loving God means keeping his commandments, and his commandments are not burdensome. For every child of God defeats this evil world, and we achieve this victory through our faith."
1 John 5:3-4 (NLT)

Day 3 — 'Your Life Has Meaning'

Daily Inspiration

Your life should matter to you first. Do not allow yourself to be deprived of fairness, grace, or justice. You were created with significance. Your life has meaning. Never conform to other people's terms when those terms do not line up with your values.

Life Application

Today is the day to discover your life significance. Connect with people who understand your rhythm and are willing to accept your desire to be you. Pursue relationships with people that share your values and beliefs.

Biblical Reflection

*" I will praise thee; for I am fearfully and
wonderfully made: marvellous are thy
works; and that my soul knoweth right
well."*

Psalm 139:14 (KJV)

Day 4 – 'The Power of Choice'

The vulnerabilities of life bring about reckless, careless, and dangerous behaviors. Life circumstances and decisions can often cause you to be easily wounded or hurt. You should believe in you enough to give yourself the choice to make appropriate decisions. Doing what is best for you is essential to your own self-development. Surround yourself with people who motivate you and encourage positive change. You are responsible for your circle.

Life Application

Decide today to avail yourself to 'The Power of Choice'. Being responsible for your circle means that not everybody can be your friend. Be selective! Choose relationships with people you enjoy, people who are good for you, and people who add value to your life.

Biblical Reflection
"Do not be misled: "Bad company corrupts good character."
1 Corinthians 15:33 (NIV)

Day 5 – 'I've Got the Power'

Daily Inspiration

Challenges and adversities are a part of life. Consequently, you must allow God's strength to stand up in you against every challenge. God will give you the grace, the power, and the strength to easily move through difficult situations. Do not attempt to work through these situations all at once. Focus on today; celebrating one victory at a time!

Life Application

Let courage be the instrument used to overcome the adversities of life. You have the power to turn your life around. Use the power created in you by God. Today, begin to declare: "I'VE GOT THE POWER!"

Biblical Reflection

"And he said unto me, My grace is sufficient for thee: for my strength is made perfect in weakness. Most gladly therefore will I rather glory in my infirmities, that the power of Christ may rest upon me."
2 Corinthians 12:9 (KJV)

Day 6 – 'Take Time to Construct You'

Daily Inspiration

Work is the essence of self-fulfillment.
Where you invest your time shows what is
most important in your life. Take time to
construct you.

Life Application

On this day, establish personal work ethics
that are in alignment with your belief
system. Make good use of your time. Focus
on activities that increase your productivity
and generate self-improvement. Time is
placed where your mind is positioned.
Maximize the moment!

Biblical Reflection

"...greater is he that is in you, than he that is in the world."
1 John 4:4 (KJV)

Day 7 – 'Rise Up'

While the enemy is plotting, God is working. He has already assured your victory. Rise up like a warrior and win! Champions are destined to succeed!

Life Application

On this day, allow the winner inside of you to meet every challenge. Stand up for what you believe and continue to focus on your dreams. Do not focus on what you do not have. Focus on what is coming. If God said it, trust that it will come to pass.

Biblical Reflection

*"So shall they fear the name of the L*ORD*
from the west, and his glory from the rising
of the sun. When the enemy shall come in
like a flood, the Spirit of the L*ORD *shall lift
up a standard against him."
Isaiah 59:19 (KJV)*

Day 8 – 'I Can Do Better'

Daily Inspiration

In the book of Genesis, Pharaoh is depicted as a taskmaster and terrorist. The modern day Pharaoh is designed to keep a grip on your faith, family, finances, fitness, and future. He must take his hands off and let you go.

Life Application

This day declare: "Pharaoh is exterminated and change is happening for me at this very moment! I believe I can do better!"

Biblical Reflection

"And Jethro said, Blessed be the LORD, who hath delivered you out of the hand of the Egyptians, and out of the hand of Pharaoh, who hath delivered the people from under the hand of the Egyptians."
Exodus 18:10 (KJV)

Day 9 – 'Dream Again'

Waiting on others to do things for you is detrimental to self-development. Now is the time to do things for yourself. Take your power back and dream again!

Life Application

This day, awaken the dreams inside of you. You have the ability to get your degree, produce your cd, start your business, write your book, and pursue whatever dream is inside of you. Avert procrastination! Take the first step toward your dreams today and do not stop until they have been accomplished!

Biblical Reflection

"I can do all things through Christ which
strengtheneth me."
Philippians 4:13 (KJV)

Day 10 – 'Stay Connected to Christ'

Daily Inspiration

The secret to living is staying connected to Christ. Those who are connected are entitled to His benefits. Rest assured that the best is yet to come.

Life Application

Dare to latch on to faith and reap the benefits of abundant living. Abundant living starts with making a decision to live for Christ. Living for Christ gives us access to immeasurable favor which leads the way to immeasurable faith. Choose Christ today and stay connected.

Biblical Reflection

"The thief cometh not, but for to steal, and to kill, and to destroy: I am come that they might have life, and that they might have it more abundantly."

John 10:10 (KJV) `

Day 11 – 'Pray Without Ceasing'

Daily Inspiration

Seasons of stagnation prevent proper development, growth, and maturity. The old season has expired. This season is meant for you to emerge and evolve.

Life Application

As part of your growth and development, practice the discipline of prayer and solitude. Avoid granting access to individuals who keep you stuck in your past and keep your present perplexed.

Biblical Reflection
"Pray without ceasing."
1 Thessalonians 5:17 (KJV)

Day 12 – 'Obsessed with Success'

Daily Inspiration

Investing in your mind causes stimulation,
inspiration, and motivation. Eventually, your
capacity for success increases. Become
obsessed with success.

Life Application

This day, begin to utilize resources and
develop relationships that will help
invigorate your mind. Invest in motivational
reading material and absorb from the energy
of therapeutic activities and healthy
relationships that improve your emotional,
psychological, and physical well-being.

Biblical Reflection

Wisdom is the principal thing; therefore get wisdom: and with all thy getting get understanding.
Proverbs 4:7 (KJV)

Day 13 – 'Positivity vs. Instability'

Daily Inspiration

Instability is a result of a disorder of the mind. Bringing order to your mind guarantees order in your life.

Life Application

Today, accept positive individuals that will provide you with mental maintenance. Accept them by defying the fears of past failures and broken relationships. These positive people may not look, act, or think like you. However, their connection to you will stimulate positive measures of stability, security, and success.

Biblical Reflection
"For who hath known the mind of the Lord,
that he may instruct him? But we have the
mind of Christ."
1 Corinthians 2:16 (KJV)

Day 14 – 'Thinking for a Change'

Daily Inspiration

A change in your thinking will solidify a change in your ways. Right thinking is beneficial for healthy living. Day to day operations of life bring us to pondering and wandering where we will discover that living is a mind thing.

Life Application

Today is the day to repent, revoke, renounce, and replace every negative thought that has produced ineffective ways, habits, and decisions. Surround yourself with innovative and creative people who will inundate you with cutting edge thinking.

Biblical Reflection

*"For as he thinketh in his heart, so is he:
Eat and drink, saith he to thee; but his heart
is not with thee."*
Proverbs 23:7 (KJV)

Day 15 – 'Intentional'

Daily Inspiration

The hand of God is like a compass that guides us through life's extreme extremities. Allow the Lord to lead and guide you along the way.

Life Application

Today, surrender to the leading of the Holy Spirit. Remove yourself from the equation and allow His leading to be your new normal. Be intentional about saying "YES!" to His will.

Biblical Reflection

"Trust in the LORD with all thine heart;
and lean not unto thine own
understanding."
Proverbs 3:5 (KJV)

Day 16 – 'The Champion in You'

Daily Inspiration

The champion in you is birthed from the challenges you endured and overcame. You possess the potential to win. Be determined to establish your life. Attention to faith, favor, and focus must become top priority.

Life Application

Today, list what is priority and set goals to secure what is most important. It will not be easy but you can do it! Distract distractions, ignore idiocy, starve stagnation, and disarm disturbances!

Biblical Reflection

"Nay, in all these things we are more than conquerors through him that loved us."
Romans 8:37 (KJV)

Day 17 – 'How Valuable Are You?'

Daily Inspiration

How are you living with what you have been given? 'The Art of Living' requires that you know your value and your worth. The value you place on yourself determines your self-worth. How valuable are you to you?

Life Application

No longer accept anything that causes you to be devalued. Obscurity becomes obsolete. Increase your value by renovating and remodeling your life. It is dire to gut out old thought patterns, emotional baggage, suppressed hurt, and live in the here and now.

Biblical Reflection

For thou hast possessed my reins: thou hast covered me in my mother's womb. I will praise thee; for I am fearfully and wonderfully made: marvellous are thy works; and that my soul knoweth right well. My substance was not hid from thee, when I was made in secret, and curiously wrought in the lowest parts of the earth. Thine eyes did see my substance, yet being unperfect; and in thy book all my members were written, which in continuance were fashioned, when as yet there was none of them.
Psalm 139:13-16 (KJV)

Day 18 – 'Finish Strong'

Daily Inspiration

There are many pieces that must be put together. Fitness for life requires stamina, perseverance, tenacity, endurance, and courage.
Rise to the occasion, connect all of the pieces, and finish Strong!

Life Application

Today, repeat the following personal pledge of allegiance: "I will confront every obstacle knowing that I am more than a conqueror. I possess the stamina to leap over every hurdle. I will stretch, I will pace, and I will abide by the rules of life. I am determined to clinch success.
I AM READY! I AM SET! I AM GONE!!!!"

Biblical Reflection
*"I press toward the mark for the prize of the
high calling of God in Christ Jesus."
Philippians 3:14 (KJV)*

Day 19 – 'Don't Waste Your Thoughts'

Daily Inspiration

Do not waste your thoughts. Assure they are retained in your mind so your life will be constructive and productive. Live your life based on purpose.

Life Application

It is vitally important to retrieve and recover every piece of your mind that was given to those who did not deserve it. Do so by never allowing yourself to get lost again in counterfeits of those who projected the image "I am for you" only to find out later that their only desire was to steal your identity. Take authority over your life by taking authority over your mind.

Biblical Reflection

"Casting down imaginations, and every high thing that exalteth itself against the knowledge of God, and bringing into captivity every thought to the obedience of Christ;"
2 Corinthians 10:5 (KJV)

Day 20 – 'Move in the Moment'

Daily Inspiration

Some moments cannot be retrieved. You must grab them while they are made available. Life can rob you of fulfillment. Capture and seize every moment.

Life Application

Move in the moment! Manage and monitor your time. The moment you are in will never be seen again. Take advantage of every opportunity to take your life back.

Biblical Reflection

Whereas ye know not what shall be on the morrow. For what is your life? It is even a vapour, that appeareth for a little time, and then vanisheth away.

James 4:14 (KJV)

Day 21 – 'Move Toward Progress'

Daily Inspiration

Unfulfilled dreams, incomplete goals, and unfinished business signify that there is still work to do. Motivation and determination is the recipe needed to move toward progress.

Life Application

Fall out of love with laziness. Only consistent people see results.

Biblical Reflection
*"The sluggard will not plow by reason of
the cold; therefore shall he beg in harvest,
and have nothing."*
Proverbs 20:4 (KJV)

Day 22 – 'Wake Up!!'

Daily Inspiration

Conflict, chaos, and catastrophe are
indicators that the giants must be eradicated
in order to enter into this new phase of life.
You are a giant slayer!
WAKE UP! WAKE UP! WAKE UP!

Life Application

Target every potential giant that poses a
threat to your success. Establish a plan of
action and reach a place of understanding.
Pray and seek the Lord and ask Him to
activate the discernment needed to recognize
any potential threats.

Biblical Reflection

"Awake, awake; put on thy strength, O Zion; put on thy beautiful garments, O Jerusalem, the holy city: for henceforth there shall no more come into thee the uncircumcised and the unclean."
Isaiah 52:1 (KJV)

Day 23 – 'The Essence of Time'

Daily Inspiration

Your journey requires movement, motion, and momentum. In order to press forward you must ascertain the essence of time. Wasting time is no longer an option.

Life Application

Understand your journey and the time factor. Listen to your internal global positioning system (GPS) and the time it takes to accomplish your dreams. Manage your time wisely.

Biblical Reflection
*"Walk in wisdom toward them that are
without, redeeming the time."*
Colossians 4:5 (KJV)

Day 24 – 'Productivity'

Daily Inspiration

Idle time promotes lack of productivity and creates procrastination. Procrastination is the enemy of progress. A productive life is pleasing to God and is the prerequisite to abundance. Productivity is the key that unlocks the door to more than just enough.

Life Application

Dismiss any false perception that interferes with the life of productivity. As you elevate your self-image, your self-esteem is also elevated. See yourself the way God sees you. False perception produces false identity.

Biblical Reflection
"The hand of the diligent shall bear rule:
but the slothful shall be under tribute."
Proverbs 12:24 (KJV)

Day 25 – 'Concentration'

Daily Inspiration

You owe it to yourself to make the
necessary adjustments for improvement.
Acquire the necessary tools that will be
beneficial to promoting growth. Growth is
assured by maintaining forward motion.
Consistency is the key to successful living.

Life Application

On this day, resume concentration that has
been easily broken. Prohibit outside
interference from dominating your decision
of total concentration! Concentration
cements the meeting of your objective.
Reserve the right to display, "DO NOT
DISTURB!"

Biblical Reflection

*And let us not be weary in well doing: for in
due season we shall reap, if we faint not.
Galatian 6:9 (KJV)*

Day 26 — 'Monitor Movements'

Daily Inspiration

'The Art of Living' requires wisdom,
instruction, and daily monitoring. It is a
masterpiece that is inclusive of the good, the
bad, and the ugly. These blended ingredients
formulate a completed design. The 'you' in
you can no longer be held hostage because
of the fear to emerge.

Life Application

Decide to monitor every movement from
this moment on. Don't rush it! Don't overdo
it! Don't exhaust yourself! It will occur!
Trust the process!

Biblical Reflection

"For God hath not given us the spirit of fear; but of power, and of love, and of a sound mind."
2 Timothy 1:7 (KJV)

Day 27 – 'Decision Day'

The opinion of your critics will sabotage the greatness of your potential. The change you desire is buried beneath your insecurity and brokenness. Escape from the place of defeat and surrender to a place of victory.

Life Application

Decision day! Will you allow the opinions of the people on the sideline to dictate how you play the game? Refer to the training in the locker room, refer to the playbook, and play your best game. Always adhere to your coaches' voice and make applicable the techniques and maneuvers he or she introduces.

Biblical Reflection

"The fear of man bringeth a snare: but whoso putteth his trust in the LORD shall be safe."

Proverbs 29:25 (KJV)

Day 28 – 'Purpose Must Be Unveiled'

Daily Inspiration

Purpose must be unveiled with knowledge
of perplexities that attach itself to frustrate
you mentally. These perplexities
unchallenged obstruct your view of the
future. Your future is eagerly awaiting your
arrival. The removal of obstacles and
hurdles is vital to reaching your destination.

Life Application

On this day accept the power of challenge
which certifies you to compete in a
competitive world. Acknowledge your fears
and insecurities; move from them and accept
them. Rebuild character and keep it moving.

Biblical Reflection
"Persecuted, but not forsaken; cast down,
but not destroyed;"
2 Corinthians 4:9 (KJV)

Day 29 – 'Conquer Every Obstacle'

Daily Inspiration

Remaining unhappy, unstable, and unfulfilled proves that one has not mastered the art of living. Barriers present themselves to contest God's plan for your life. 'Shifting' is the introduction to promoting a healthy spirit, soul, and body. In order to reach your goals your life must first matter to you.

Life Application

Trust God to give you the ability to conquer every obstacle that is before you. Placing the focus on you must become top priority. Connect with a Christian coach who will assist you in removal of obstacles that have prevented knowledge of self and motivation for change.

Biblical Reflection

"The fear of the LORD tendeth to life: and he that hath it shall abide satisfied; he shall not be visited with evil."
Proverbs 19:23 (KJV)

Day 30 – 'Occupy Until He Comes'

Daily Inspiration

God places people on earth 'in time' for a 'set time' to occupy until He comes. The question is: "What are you doing with your time?" When you respect 'time', 'time' respects you. Keep grinding toward greatness. Every closed door represents the fact that a new door is opening and the next chapter of your life is beginning. You are bold, you are bright, you are beautiful, and you are brilliant.

Life Application

No longer allow life's challenges to deter you from living because of fear of the unknown. Decide to be conscious of your life's direction. What you have endured is not the end of your story. What you have endured is the beginning of HIS story; an opportunity to learn and live. You are the equivalent to a piece of art where there is a hidden meaning and a message only for the eyes of those who know and appreciate the effort invested by the Creator to build a masterpiece like you.

Biblical Reflection

"And he called his ten servants, and delivered them ten pounds, and said unto them, Occupy till I come." Luke 19:13 (KJV)

Motivational Moment

A life based on purpose is a life worth living. Your life matters to God. Inadequacy is no longer acceptable. God uses adverse circumstances to re-image you for the future. Redesign, rebuild, and reclaim your life TODAY!

Your life matters!!!! Make it count!!!
--Terry A. Weems, Sr.

Praise for 'The Art of Living'

The art of being made up of different types of dust.
To be made into His likeness; designed to serve an
imperfect world like this.
Dreams, visions, and missions; all the essence of
self- fulfillment.
Self-improvement to become a greater instrument.
Embracing the moment to defeat the odds and
every road block that has tried to become a
hindering block.
Understanding that God hides you behind a rock.

So my motivation as I read 'The Art of Living'
thrust me to embrace the inner me
which captivates the God in me;
Giving me the fortitude to know my value and my
worth and not another dream deferred.
Stamina, perseverance, tenacity, endurance, and
courage;
all the things I need in life to let my dream be
heard.

Embracing the greatness in me and showcasing the
art that is living within me.
Rebuilding the image you see so God can get the
glory out of me.
'The Art of Living'; an inspirational.
The greatest aspiration to fulfill an empty nation.

Shide Hill

Additional resources from
Terry A. Weems Ministries
www.terryaweems.org

Shifting and Lifting: Engaging a Metamorphoo

This book describes the essence of the transitional process for the next dimension. 'Shifting and Lifting: Engaging a Metamorphoo' is empowering, enriching, refreshing, motivational, transformational, and uplifting.

'Shifting and Lifting: Engaging a Metamorphoo' is available at www.amazon.com and www.terryaweems.org.

'The Responsibility Factor' Workshop Manual

Advancing, Progressing, and Prospering

Visionary of Obadiah's Ecclesiastical Alliance

www.oealliance.org

Made in the USA
Columbia, SC
06 January 2021

30408151R00039